FORWARD/COMMENTARY

The National Institute of Standards and Technology (NIST) is a measurement standards laboratory, and a non-regulatory agency of the United States Department of Commerce. Its mission is to promote innovation and industrial competitiveness. Founded in 1901, as the National Bureau of Standards, NIST was formed with the mandate to provide standard weights and measures, and to serve as the national physical laboratory for the United States. With a world-class measurement and testing laboratory encompassing a wide range of areas of computer science, mathematics, statistics, and systems engineering, NIST's cybersecurity program supports its overall mission to promote U.S. innovation and industrial competitiveness by advancing measurement science, standards, and related technology through research and development in ways that enhance economic security and improve our quality of life.

The need for cybersecurity standards and best practices that address interoperability, usability and privacy has been shown to be critical for the nation. NIST's cybersecurity programs seek to enable greater development and application of practical, innovative security technologies and methodologies that enhance the country's ability to address current and future computer and information security challenges.

The cybersecurity publications produced by NIST cover a wide range of cybersecurity concepts that are carefully designed to work together to produce a holistic approach to cybersecurity primarily for government agencies and constitute the best practices used by industry. This holistic strategy to cybersecurity covers the gamut of security subjects from development of secure encryption standards for communication and storage of information while at rest to how best to recover from a cyber-attack.

Why buy a book you can download for free?   **We print this so you don't have to.**

Some are available only in electronic media. Some online docs are missing pages or barely legible.

We at 4th Watch Publishing are former government employees, so we know how government employees actually use the standards. When a new standard is released, an engineer prints it out, punches holes and puts it in a 3-ring binder. While this is not a big deal for a 5 or 10-page document, many NIST documents are over 100 pages and printing a large document is a time-consuming effort. So, an engineer that's paid $75 an hour is spending hours simply printing out the tools needed to do the job. That's time that could be better spent doing engineering. We publish these documents so engineers can focus on what they were hired to do – engineering. It's much more cost-effective to just order the latest version from Amazon.com

If there is a standard you would like published, let us know. Our web site is: usgovpub.com

NISTIR 7511
Revision 5

Security Content Automation Protocol (SCAP) Version 1.3 Validation Program Test Requirements

Melanie Cook
Stephen Quinn
David Waltermire
Dragos Prisaca

This publication is available free of charge from:
https://doi.org/10.6028/NIST.IR.7511r5

National Institute of
Standards and Technology
U.S. Department of Commerce

NISTIR 7511
Revision 5

Security Content Automation Protocol (SCAP) Version 1.3 Validation Program Test Requirements

Melanie Cook
Stephen Quinn
David Waltermire
Computer Security Division
Information Technology Laboratory

Dragos Prisaca
G2, Inc.
Annapolis Junction, MD

This publication is available free of charge from:
https://doi.org/10.6028/NIST.IR.7511r5

April 2018

U.S. Department of Commerce
Wilbur L. Ross, Jr., Secretary

National Institute of Standards and Technology
Walter Copan, NIST Director and Under Secretary of Commerce for Standards and Technology

National Institute of Standards and Technology Internal Report 7511 Revision 5
51 pages (April 2018)

This publication is available free of charge from:
https://doi.org/10.6028/NIST.IR.7511r5

Comments on this publication may be submitted to:

National Institute of Standards and Technology
Attn: Computer Security Division, Information Technology Laboratory
100 Bureau Drive (Mail Stop 8930), Gaithersburg, MD 20899-8930
Email: ir7511comments@nist.gov

All comments are subject to release under the Freedom of Information Act (FOIA).

Reports on Computer Systems Technology

The Information Technology Laboratory (ITL) at the National Institute of Standards and Technology (NIST) promotes the U.S. economy and public welfare by providing technical leadership for the Nation's measurement and standards infrastructure. ITL develops tests, test methods, reference data, proof of concept implementations, and technical analyses to advance the development and productive use of information technology. ITL's responsibilities include the development of management, administrative, technical, and physical standards and guidelines for the cost-effective security and privacy of other than national security-related information in federal information systems.

Abstract

This report defines the requirements and associated test procedures necessary for products or modules to achieve one or more Security Content Automation Protocol (SCAP) validations. Validation is awarded based on a defined set of SCAP capabilities by independent laboratories that have been accredited for SCAP testing by the NIST National Voluntary Laboratory Accreditation Program (NVLAP).

Keywords

Security Content Automation Protocol (SCAP); SCAP derived test requirements (DTR); SCAP validated tools; SCAP validated products; SCAP validated modules; SCAP validation

Acknowledgements

The authors, Melanie Cook, Stephen Quinn, and David Waltermire of the National Institute of Standards and Technology (NIST), and Dragos Prisaca of G2, Inc. would like to thank the many people who reviewed and contributed to this document, in particular, John Banghart of Venable LLP who was the original author and pioneered the first SCAP Validation Program. The authors thank Matt Kerr, and Danny Haynes of the MITRE Corporation for their insightful technical contribution to the design of the SCAP 1.2 Validation Program and creation of the first revision of SCAP 1.2 validation test content which is the basis for the SCAP 1.3 validation program.

The authors would like to acknowledge the following reviewers of this document for their keen and insightful assistance: Joshua Lubell and Celia Paulsen of NIST.

Audience

This publication is intended for NVLAP accredited laboratories conducting SCAP product and module testing for the program, vendors interested in receiving SCAP validation for their products or modules, and organizations deploying SCAP products in their environments. Accredited laboratories use the information in this report to guide their testing and ensure all necessary requirements are met by a product before recommending to NIST that the product be awarded the requested validation. Vendors may use the information in this report to understand the features that products and modules need to be considered for SCAP validation. Government agencies and integrators use the information to gain insight into the criteria required for SCAP validated products. The secondary audience for this publication includes end users, who can review the test requirements to understand the capabilities of SCAP validated products and gain knowledge about SCAP validation.

Trademark Information

OVAL is a trademark of the US Department of Homeland Security (DHS).

CVE is a registered trademark of The MITRE Corporation.

Red Hat, Red Hat Enterprise Linux and Red Hat Linux are registered trademarks of Red Hat, Inc.

Windows operating systems are registered trademarks of Microsoft Corporation.

Mac and OS X are trademarks of Apple Inc.

All other registered trademarks or trademarks belong to their respective organizations.

Summary of Changes

The following table details the changes between NISTIR 7511 Revision 4 and NISTIR 7511 Revision 5, which are incorporated in the present document.

Date	Type	Change	Page Number
04/20/2018	Editorial	Sorted the items listed in Appendix A in alphabetical order	37
04/20/2018	Editorial	Corrected the section number referenced by SCAP.V.2500.1	22
04/20/2018	Substantive	Updated the SCAP.T.2860.1 to match the requirement SCAP.R.2860	24
04/20/2018	Editorial	Updated the status of the SP800-126r3, SP800-126A, and SP800-70 to 'Final'	43
04/20/2018	Substantive	Replaced "Schematron style sheets" with "Schematron schemas" to match ISO 19757-3 terminology throughout the document	n/a
04/20/2018	Substantive	Updated SCAP.T.1300.2 to include both XSD and Schematron schema for XCCDF component validation.	15
04/20/2018	Editorial	Corrected a bookmark error related to "Added Software Identification (SWID) Tags 2015 revision" in this table	iv
04/20/2018	Editorial	Corrected superscript typo "metadata7"	5
04/20/2018	Substantive	Deleted the following footnote: "In cases where there are no USGCB source data streams applicable to the tested platform, this requirement does not apply." from requirement SCAP.R.1500	16
04/20/2018	Substantive	Added the text "If there are no USGCB source data streams for the platform(s) being tested, then this requirement is not applicable." to requirement SCAP.R.1500	16
04/20/2018	Substantive	Updated R.1100 to clarify what legacy versions of content are supported	14
04/20/2018	Editorial	Corrected the link to [OMB M-08-22]	43
04/20/2018	Editorial	Changed the revision of the document from "4" to "5" throughout the document	n/a
04/20/2018	Editorial	Updated the release date throughout the document	n/a
04/20/2018	Editorial	Updated SCAP version to 1.3 throughout the document	n/a
04/20/2018	Editorial	Updated the URL of this publication throughout the document	n/a
04/20/2018	Editorial	Updated the NIST URLs to use https instead http throughout the document	n/a
04/20/2018	Editorial	Updated the "Trademark Information" section	iv
04/20/2018	Editorial	Updated the "Acknowledgements" section	iv
04/20/2018	Editorial	Updated the "Table of Contents" to reflect the changes throughout the document	n/a
04/20/2018	Substantive	Added the name of the Appendices in the section "Introduction"	2
04/20/2018	Substantive	Removed previous superseded programs in section "Superseded Validation Programs"	3
04/20/2018	Substantive	Updated section "2. SCAP 1.2 Component Specification Versions" to include the SCAP 1.3 specifications and removed sub-sections 2.1 – 2.12	4
04/20/2018	Substantive	Added Software Identification (SWID) Tags 2015 revision	5
04/20/2018	Substantive	Removed references to SCAP Interpreter and "reference implementation" from section "SCAP Validation Tools"	9
04/20/2018	Editorial	Removed example from sub-section 3.2	8
04/20/2018	Editorial	Merged sub-section 3.3.1 into 3.3	9
04/20/2018	Substantive	Deleted section "3.3.2 Reference implementation tools"	n/a

Date	Type	Change	Page Number
04/20/2018	Substantive	Added a new requirement SCAP.R.900	14
04/20/2018	Substantive	Added additional sub-requirements to SCAP.R.1300	15
04/20/2018	Substantive	Added clarification about OCIL component validations to SCAP.R.1400	16
04/20/2018	Substantive	Updated SCAP.T.1510.1 to check patches up-to-date XCCDF rule implemented via multiple OVAL definitions	17
04/20/2018	Substantive	Added sub-requirements SCAP.T.1510.2 to check patches up-to-date XCCDF rule implemented via a single OVAL definition	17
04/20/2018	Substantive	Removed references to NCP Tiers from requirement SCAP.R.1700	18
04/20/2018	Editorial	Replaced "file" with "component" to comply with SCAP 1.3 terminology for requirement SCAP.R.2000	19
04/20/2018	Editorial	Replaced "file" with "component" to comply with SCAP 1.3 terminology for requirement SCAP.R.2200	20
04/20/2018	Editorial	SCAP.R.2700: Updated URL to CVE ID	23
04/20/2018	Substantive	Added a new requirement SCAP.R.2850	24
04/20/2018	Substantive	Added a new requirement SCAP.R.2860	24
04/20/2018	Substantive	Added new sub-requirements SCAP.T.2900.1 and SCAP.T.2900.2	25
04/20/2018	Substantive	Added all valid results to SCAP.R.3000	27
04/20/2018	Substantive	Added clarification about the source content used for scanning to SCAP.R.3400	30
04/20/2018	Substantive	Added a new sub-requirement SCAP.T.3400.2	30
04/20/2018	Substantive	Removed requirement SCAP.R.4600	34
04/20/2018	Substantive	Updated Appendix D: removed references to NCP Tiers; added new references	42

Table of Contents

1. Introduction

The National Institute of Standards and Technology (NIST) Security Content Automation Protocol (SCAP) Validation Program tests the ability of products and modules to use the features and functionality available through SCAP and its components. SCAP 1.3 consists of a suite of specifications for standardizing the format and nomenclature by which security software communicates information about software flaws and security configurations. The standardization of security information facilitates interoperability and enables predictable results among disparate SCAP enabled security software. The SCAP Validation Program provides vendors an opportunity to have independent verification that security software correctly processes SCAP expressed security information and provides standardized output. Industry and government end users benefit from the SCAP Validation Program by having assurance that SCAP validated products have undergone independent testing and met all requirements defined in this document.

The validation program supports the U.S. Office of Management and Budget (OMB) Memorandum M-08-22 to Federal CIOs [OMB M-08-22]. This memorandum states, "Both industry and government information technology providers must use SCAP validated tools with FDCC [Federal Desktop Core Configuration] Scanner capability to certify their products operate correctly with FDCC configurations and do not alter FDCC settings. Agencies will use SCAP tools to scan for both FDCC configurations and configuration deviations approved by department or agency accrediting authority. Agencies must also use these tools when monitoring use of these configurations as part of FISMA [Federal Information Security Management Act] continuous monitoring."[1] The checklist portion of the FDCC mandate is now referred to as the United States Government Configuration Baseline (USGCB), and the FDCC Scanner capability has evolved and is now referred to as the Authenticated Configuration Scanner (ACS) capability.[2]

Under the SCAP Validation Program, independent laboratories are accredited by the NIST National Voluntary Laboratory Accreditation Program (NVLAP). Accreditation requirements are defined in NIST Handbook 150, *National Voluntary Laboratory Accreditation Program: Procedures and General Requirements* [NIST HB 150] and NIST Handbook 150-17, *NVLAP Cryptographic and Security Testing* [NIST HB 150-17]. More information about NVLAP can be found at https://www.nist.gov/nvlap/.

Independent laboratories conduct the tests defined in this document on products at the request of vendors and deliver the results to NIST. Based on the independent laboratory test report, the SCAP Validation Program then validates the product under test. The validation certificates awarded to vendor products are publicly posted on the NIST SCAP Validated Products web page (https://csrc.nist.gov/projects/scap-validation-program/validated-products-and-modules).[3] An information technology (IT) vendor can obtain multiple validations for a product. For example, a vendor may choose to validate on one platform and then validate additional platforms later. Products are validated in the context of a particular SCAP capability.[4]

An SCAP product is defined as a software application that has one or more capabilities. An SCAP module is defined as an embedded software component of a product or application, or a complete product in-and-of-itself that has one or more capabilities. Unless otherwise stated herein, the term "implementation under test (IUT)" refers to either a "product" or "module" under test.

---

[1]   [OMB M-08-22, p.2]
[2]   https://usgcb.nist.gov
[3]   The SCAP Validation Program does not provide physical certificates to the participating vendors.
[4]   The SCAP Validation Program defines SCAP capability as "a specific function or functions of a product or module." Further information can be found in Section 3.

1.1 Purpose and Scope

The purpose of this report is to define the SCAP 1.3 Validation Program Derived Test Requirements. This report gives an introduction to the SCAP 1.3 Validation Program and documents the requirements for SCAP 1.3 product and module validations. Future versions of the SCAP Validation Program will be defined in revisions of this report, each labeled with a revision number and the appropriate SCAP version number.

1.2 Document Structure

The remainder of this document is organized into the following major sections:
- Section 2 describes SCAP and its component specification versions referenced in the SCAP 1.3 validation program,
- Section 3 describes the validation process,
- Section 4 defines the derived test requirements,
- Section 5 maps the derived test requirements to SCAP capabilities,
- Appendix A—Terms and Definitions lists terms and definitions,
- Appendix B—Acronyms lists acronyms,
- Appendix C—Use of SCAP 1.3 Logo and phrases discusses the use of the SCAP 1.3 logo and phrases, and
- Appendix D—References includes a list of references.

1.3 Document Conventions

Throughout this document, the key words "MUST", "MUST NOT", "REQUIRED", "SHALL", "SHALL NOT", "SHOULD", "SHOULD NOT", "RECOMMENDED", "MAY", and "OPTIONAL" in this document are to be interpreted as described in the Internet Engineering Task Force (IETF) Request for Comments (RFC) 2119 [RFC 2119].

Some of the requirements and conventions used in this document reference Extensible Markup Language (XML) content [XMLS]. These references come in two forms, inline and indented. An example of an inline reference is: a `<cpe2_dict:cpe-item>` may contain `<cpe2_dict:check>` elements that reference OVAL Definitions[5].

In this example the notation `<cpe2_dict:cpe-item>` can be replaced by the more verbose equivalent "the XML element whose qualified name is `cpe2_dict:cpe-item`".

An example of an indented reference is:

References to OVAL Definitions are expressed using the following format:

```
<cpe2_dict:check system=
"http://oval.mitre.org/XMLSchema/oval-definitions-5"
href="Oval_URL">[Oval_inventory_definition_id]
</cpe2_dict:check>.
```

The general convention used when describing XML attributes within this document is to reference the attribute as well as its associated element including the namespace alias, employing the general form `"@attributeName` for the `<prefix:localName>"`.

---

[5] An OVAL Definition is a standardized check for expressing a specific machine state.

Indented references are intended to represent the form of actual XML content. Indented references represent literal content by the use of a `fixed-length font`, and parametric (freely replaceable) content by the use of an *italic font*. Square brackets ' `[]` ' are used to designate optional content. Thus "`[`*Oval_inventory_definition_id*`]`" designates optional parametric content.

Both inline and indented forms use qualified names to refer to specific XML elements. A qualified name associates a named element with a namespace. The namespace identifies the XML model, and the XML schema is a definition and implementation of that model. A qualified name declares this schema to element association using the format '*prefix:element-name*'. The association of prefix to namespace is defined in the metadata of an XML document and varies from document to document. In this specification, the conventional mappings listed in Table 1-1. are used.

Table 1-1. Conventional XML Mappings[6]

Prefix	Namespace	Schema
cpe2	http://cpe.mitre.org/language/2.0	Embedded CPE references
cpe2-dict	http://cpe.mitre.org/dictionary/2.0	CPE dictionaries
xccdf	http://checklists.nist.gov/xccdf/1.2	XCCDF policy documents
xml	http://www.w3.org/XML/1998/namespace	Common XML attributes

1.4   Superseded Validation Programs

This publication supersedes the *Security Content Automation Protocol (SCAP) Version 1.2 Validation Program Test Requirements* revision 4. The previous revisions of the program for SCAP 1.0 and 1.1 have been also deprecated.

---

[6] For a complete list of mappings, please refer to [NIST SP 800-126 R3].

2. SCAP 1.3 Component Specification Versions

For all test requirements that reference particular specifications, the versions indicated in this section SHOULD be used and are derived primarily from the SCAP 1.3 as defined in NIST Special Publication (SP) 800-126 Revision 3 [NIST SP 800-126 R3] and as updated by NIST Special Publication 800-126A [NIST SP 800-126A].

SCAP is a suite of specifications established by NIST for expressing and manipulating security data in standardized ways. Adoption of SCAP facilitates an organization's automation of continuous monitoring, vulnerability management, and security policy compliance evaluation reporting.

The component specifications that comprise SCAP 1.3 are as follows:

- Extensible Configuration Checklist Description Format (XCCDF) 1.2, an Extensible Markup Language (XML) specification for structured collections of security configuration rules used by operating system (OS) and application platforms [XCCDF];

  Schema Location: https://scap.nist.gov/schema/xccdf/1.2/xccdf_1.2.xsd

- Open Vulnerability and Assessment Language (OVAL), an XML specification for exchanging technical details on how to check systems for security-related software flaws, configuration issues, and software patches [OVAL] [7];

  Schema Location: https://github.com/OVALProject/Language/tree/5.11.2/schemas

- Open Checklist Interactive Language (OCIL) 2.0, a language for representing checks that collect information from people or from existing data stores made by other data collection efforts [OCIL];

  Schema Location: https://scap.nist.gov/schema/ocil/2.0/ocil-2.0.xsd

- Common Configuration Enumeration (CCE) 5, a dictionary of names for software security configuration issues (e.g., access control settings, password policy settings) [CCE];

  Dictionary: https://nvd.nist.gov/config/cce/index

- Common Platform Enumeration (CPE) 2.3, a naming convention for hardware, OS, and application products [CPE];

  CPE.Naming
  Definition: The Naming specification defines the logical structure of Well-Formed Names (WFNs).
  Schema Location: https://scap.nist.gov/schema/cpe/2.3/cpe-naming_2.3.xsd

  CPE.Name Matching
  Definition: The Name Matching specification defines the procedures for comparing WFNs to each other with the purpose of determining whether they refer to some or all of the same products.

  CPE.Dictionary
  Definition: The Dictionary specification defines the concept of a CPE dictionary, which is a repository of CPE names and metadata, with each name identifying a single class of IT product. The Dictionary specification defines processes for using the dictionary, such as how to search for a particular CPE name or look for dictionary entries that belong to a broader product class. Also, the

---

[7] See the Table 2: Approved OVAL Platform Schema Versions of the SCAP 1.3 annex document, [NIST SP 800-126A], for the OVAL component specification (core schema) versions and platform schema versions that are supported by SCAP 1.3.

Dictionary specification outlines all the rules that dictionary maintainers MUST follow when creating new dictionary entries and updating existing entries.

Schema Locations: https://scap.nist.gov/schema/cpe/2.3/cpe-dictionary_2.3.xsd
                    https://scap.nist.gov/schema/cpe/2.3/cpe-dictionary-extension_2.3.xsd

CPE.Applicability LanguageDefinition: The Applicability Language specification defines a standardized structure for forming complex logical expressions out of WFNs. These expressions, also known as applicability statements, are used to tag checklists, policies, guidance, and other documents with information about the product(s) to which the documents apply.
Schema Location: https://scap.nist.gov/schema/cpe/2.3/cpe-language_2.3.xsd

- Software Identification (SWID) Tags 2015 revision, a format for representing software identifiers and associated metadata[8] [SWID];

  Version: ISO/IEC 19770-2:2015 published in October 2015

  Schema Location: http://standards.iso.org/iso/19770/-2/2015/schema.xsd

- Common Vulnerabilities and Exposures (CVE), a dictionary of names for publicly known security-related software flaws[9] [CVE];

  Specification: http://cve.mitre.org/

- Common Vulnerability Scoring System (CVSS) 3.0, a method for classifying characteristics of software flaws and assigning severity scores based on these characteristics [CVSS];

  CVSS Base Scores: https://nvd.nist.gov/

- Common Configuration Scoring System (CCSS) 1.0, a system for measuring the relative severity of system security configuration issues [CCSS];

- Asset Identification 1.1, a format for uniquely identifying assets based on known identifiers and/or known information about the assets [AI];

  Schema Location: https://scap.nist.gov/schema/asset-identification/1.1/asset-identification_1.1.0.xsd

- Asset Reporting Format (ARF) 1.1, a format for expressing the transport format of information about assets and the relationships between assets and reports [ARF]; and

  Schema Location: https://scap.nist.gov/schema/asset-reporting-format/1.1/asset-reporting-format_1.1.0.xsd

- Trust Model for Security Automation Data (TMSAD) 1.0, a specification for using digital signatures in a common trust model applied to other security automation specifications [TMSAD].

  Schema Location: https://scap.nist.gov/schema/tmsad/1.0/tmsad_1.0.xsd

The SCAP specification describes the SCAP components at a high level and how the components relate to each other within the context of SCAP. The SCAP specification does not define the SCAP components in detail; each component has its own standalone specification document or reference. The SCAP components were created and are maintained by several entities, including NIST, the MITRE

---

[8] The "2015 revision" refers to ISO/IEC 19770-2:2015, which is the specification for SWID tags
[9] CVE does not have a version number.

Corporation, the National Security Agency (NSA), and the Forum of Incident Response and Security Teams (FIRST).

NIST provides security data feeds, such as vulnerability and product enumeration identifiers, through a repository supplied by the National Vulnerability Database (NVD).[10] SCAP security checklists or benchmarks created by NIST or other organizations are also made available by through the National Checklist Program (NCP).[11] The content in the NVD and NCP repositories is freely available. More information about SCAP can be found at https://csrc.nist.gov/projects/scap.

---

[10] https://nvd.nist.gov
[11] https://checklists.nist.gov

3. Validation Process

With the SCAP Validation Program, NVLAP-accredited laboratories conduct the tests defined in this document on products and deliver the test report to NIST. NIST reviews the test report and determines whether the product has successfully fulfilled all requirements for SCAP validation. Upon successful completion of all requirements, the NIST SCAP Validation Program then validates the product based on the independent laboratory test report. SCAP validated products and modules are publicly posted on the NIST SCAP Validated Products web page at https://csrc.nist.gov/projects/scap-validation-program/validated-products-and-modules.

This section of the document covers the validation process. Section 3.1 discusses SCAP 1.3 capabilities and validations. Section 3.2 addresses demarcation and validation expirations. Finally, Section 3.3 discusses SCAP Validation tools.

3.1 SCAP 1.3 Capabilities and Validations

Vendors may seek product validation for one core and two optional SCAP 1.3 capabilities on one or more platform such as those listed below.

SCAP Capabilities

- Authenticated Configuration Scanner (ACS) core SCAP 1.3 capability
  - CVE option (optional CVE support MAY be combined with ACS)
  - OCIL option (optional OCIL support MAY be combined with ACS)

CVE and OCIL are optional SCAP component specifications that MAY be combined with ACS in SCAP 1.3 product validations. Product vendors MAY elect adding CVE, OCIL, or both options to the core ACS product validation. If the CVE option is chosen, the product MUST pass all CVE requirements marked in the CVE column in Table 5-1. If the OCIL option is chosen, the product must pass all OCIL requirements marked in the OCIL column in Table 5-1. Products may not be validated against the CVE or OCIL requirements alone. These optional validations MUST be combined with the core ACS product validation.

The list of OVAL tests used for testing the ACS SCAP 1.3 capability is published on the SCAP Validation Program web page https://csrc.nist.gov/projects/scap-validation-program.[12]

NOTE: The ACS capability includes the FDCC Scanner functionality that is mentioned in Office of Management and Budget (OMB) memorandum M-08-22, *Guidance on the Federal Desktop Core Configuration (FDCC)* [OMB M-08-22] and the USGCB Scanner previously offered in the SCAP 1.0 validation program.

Platforms

NIST reserves the right to add or remove platforms in future updates to the SCAP 1.3 Validation Program. The platforms supported at the release of this document included several versions of Microsoft Windows, Red Hat Enterprise Linux, and Mac OS. The SCAP Validation Program may add support for

---

[12] Support of deprecated OVAL tests is required for the Authenticated Configuration Scanner (ACS) capability. Backward compatibility is required for SCAP 1.3 validated products.

new platforms which will be listed on the SCAP Validation Program web page. For the most current list of available platforms, please refer to https://csrc.nist.gov/projects/scap-validation-program.

Validations will be awarded to major version of the product or module for SCAP capabilities and supported platform(s). Vendors MUST provide a description of their product versioning method in order to define how major releases are numbered for the product entering the validation process. In general, validations will be awarded to major releases of products; however, if a minor release modifies the SCAP component of the product, then the vendor SHOULD validate the minor release. Validated products will be listed on the SCAP Validated Products and Modules web page and will include the following information:

- Product/module vendor or manufacturer name,
- Product/module name,
- Product/module major version validated,
- Product/module version tested (full identifier at the time of testing),
- Platforms tested,
- SCAP Capabilities,
- Validation number,
- Validation date,
- Validation test suite version used for testing, and
- NVLAP lab number.

3.2   Demarcation and Validation Expirations

The SCAP Validation Program recognizes the need for a clear demarcation point for end users, product vendors, the standards body and NVLAP accredited labs in order to develop, test, and deploy efficiently. The SCAP Validation Program also recognizes that SCAP component specifications, standards, and products typically change over time and employ a variety of versioning schemes for identifying different releases.

The final release date of NISTIR 7511 for the next major version of SCAP[13] determines the end of SCAP 1.3 validations and the expiration date for SCAP 1.3 product validations.

- The SCAP Validation Program will stop accepting SCAP 1.3 test submissions 15 months after the final release of NISTIR 7511 for the next SCAP major version as defined in SP 800-126.
- SCAP 1.3 product validations will expire 12 months after the SCAP Validation Program stops accepting SCAP 1.3 test submissions.[14]

This document identifies a specific set of SCAP component specifications as described in Section 2 and the associated Derived Test Requirements (DTRs) as described in Section 4. Minor SCAP version updates defined by SP 800-126A are reflected in validation test suite updates and are included as part of the product validation information posted on the https://csrc.nist.gov/projects/scap-validation-program/validated-products-and-modules web page.

Minor updates to SCAP 1.3 component specifications as defined in SP 800-126A and product updates do not invalidate SCAP 1.3 validated products. Vendors may choose to revalidate products based on a change to SP 800-126A, for example if a new OVAL test is added to an OVAL platform schema. Major

---

[13]   The current version of SCAP is 1.3. Major versions are defined in SP 800-126. Minor version updates of component specifications already included in an SCAP major version are defined in SP 800-126A.

[14]   See https://scap.nist.gov/timeline.html for more information about the SCAP release cycle.

changes in product functionality, including support for new SCAP technologies, may require product revalidation.

3.3   SCAP Validation Tools

The SCAP Validation Program uses several tools that aid in the development and testing of SCAP products. One of them is the SCAP Validation (SCAPVal) Tool that may be used for checking SCAP source and results data streams for conformance to SCAP specifications. The output results from SCAPVal are required during formal SCAP validation testing.
The SCAP Validation Tool (SCAPVal) validates the conformance of an SCAP data stream to a particular use case according to what is defined in SP 800-126 and SP 800-126A. The SCAPVal output provides information about whether an SCAP data stream conforms to conventions and recommendations outlined in SP 800-126 Rev. 3 [NIST SP 800-126 R3] and SP 800-126A.

SCAPVal provides the following functions:
- Validates the data stream according to one of the use cases for an SCAP-validated product listed in Section 5 of [NIST SP 800-126 R3], namely Compliance Checking, Vulnerability Scanning, or Inventory Scanning.
- Checks components and data streams against appropriate schemas.
- Uses Schematron to perform additional checks within and across component data streams.
- Produces XML and HTML validation results that convey all error and warning conditions detected.

For a listing of the SCAP requirements, refer to the SCAP Version 1.1 Requirements Matrix, SCAP Version 1.2 Requirements Matrix, and SCAP Version 1.3 Requirements Matrix included with the tool. SCAPVal may be downloaded from https://scap.nist.gov/revision/1.3/ .

4.   Derived Test Requirements (DTR)

This section contains the test requirements for each of the SCAP components for the purpose of allowing individual validation of each SCAP component within a product. Version information and download location, listed in Section 2, SHOULD be referenced to ensure that the correct version is being used prior to testing. SCAP-specific requirements are found in Section 5.

Each DTR includes the following information:

- The DTR name: comprised of the acronym followed by ".R" to denote it is a requirement, and then the requirement number.

- SCAP Capability (summarized in Table 5-1) where

    o   ACS = Authenticated Configuration Scanner

        o   CVE = Optional CVE Support when combined with ACS

        o   OCIL = Optional OCIL Support when combined with ACS.

- Required vendor information: comprised of the acronym followed by ".V" to denote that it is vendor information, then states required information vendors MUST provide to the testing lab for the test to be conducted.

- Required test procedure(s): comprised of the acronym followed by ".T" to denote that it is a test procedure, then defines one or more tests that the testing laboratory will conduct to determine the product's ability to meet the stated requirement.

The derived test requirements are organized into the following major categories:

1. **Assertions** – Statements made by the vendor (in its documentation) that indicate what the product does (or does not) do relative to SCAP and its components (see Section 4.1)

2. **Input Processing and Correctness** – Those requirements that define the processing of SCAP source data streams and their major permutations (e.g., various source data stream tests such as source data streams with multiple benchmarks, legacy data streams, and signed data streams) (see Section 4.2)

3. **Results Production** – Those requirements that define how products will be assessed for their ability to produce valid SCAP results (see Section 4.3)

4.1   SCAP Assertions

This section addresses the assertions that vendors MUST make about the products seeking validations relative to SCAP and its component specifications as defined in Section 2.

SCAP.R.100: The product's documentation (printed or electronic) MUST assert that it uses SCAP and its component specifications and explain relevant details to the users of the product.

SCAP Capability: ☑ ACS   ☐ CVE   ☐ OCIL

Required Vendor Information:

SCAP.V.100.1: The vendor SHALL indicate where in the product documentation information regarding the use of SCAP and its components can be found. This MAY be a physical document or an electronic document (e.g., a PDF, help file, etc.).

Required Test Procedures:

SCAP.T.100.1: The tester SHALL visually inspect the product documentation to verify that information regarding the product's use of SCAP and its components is present and verify that the SCAP documentation is in a location accessible to any user of the product. This test does not involve judging the quality of the documentation or its accuracy.

SCAP.R.200: The vendor MUST assert that the product implements SCAP and its component specifications and provide a high-level summary of the implementation approach as well as a statement of backward compatibility with earlier versions of SCAP and related components.

SCAP Capability: ☑ ACS   ☐ CVE   ☐ OCIL

Required Vendor Information:

SCAP.V.200.1: The vendor SHALL provide to the lab a separate, 150- to 2500- word explanation written in the English language asserting that the product implements SCAP and its component specifications for the capabilities claimed in Table 5-1. This document SHALL include a high-level summary of the implementation approach and an assertion of backwards compatibility with SCAP 1.1 and SCAP 1.2. This content will be used on NIST web pages to explain details about each validated product and thus SHOULD contain only information that may be publicly released.

Required Test Procedures:

SCAP.T.200.1: The tester SHALL inspect the provided documentation to verify that the documentation asserts that the product implements SCAP and its component specifications and provides a high-level summary of the implementation approach and an assertion of backwards compatibility with SCAP 1.1 and SCAP 1.2. This test does not judge the quality or accuracy of the documentation, nor does it test how thoroughly the product implements SCAP or backwards compatibility with previous versions.

SCAP.T.200.2: The tester SHALL verify that the provided documentation is an English language document consisting of 150 to 2500 words.

SCAP.R.300: The SCAP capabilities claimed by the vendor for the product under test MUST match the scope of the product's asserted capabilities for the target platform.

    SCAP Capability: ☑ ACS   ☐ CVE   ☐ OCIL

    Required Vendor Information:

    SCAP.V.300.1: The vendor SHALL indicate the defined SCAP capabilities (one or more) for which their product is being tested.

    Required Test Procedures:

    SCAP.T.300.1: The tester SHALL ensure that all tests associated with the asserted SCAP capabilities of the product are conducted.

    SCAP.T.300.2: The tester SHALL review product documentation to ensure that the product has implemented the SCAP capabilities for which it is being tested (e.g., Authenticated Configuration Scanner).

4.2 SCAP Source Data Stream Processing and Correctness

This section addresses the ability of a product to correctly process SCAP source data streams.

SCAP.R.400: The product SHALL be able to import SCAP source data streams for the target platform and correctly load the included Rules and their associated Check System Definitions, rejecting any invalid content.

    SCAP Capability: ☑ ACS   ☐ CVE   ☐ OCIL

    Required Vendor Information:

    SCAP.V.400.1: The vendor SHALL provide documentation and instruction on how to import SCAP source data streams for the target platform.

    Required Test Procedures:

    SCAP.T.400.1: The tester SHALL import valid SCAP source data streams for the target platform into the vendor product and execute the data streams on a target system. Results of the scan SHALL be inspected to ensure actual results match expected results.

    SCAP.T.400.2: The tester SHALL import an invalid SCAP source data stream into the vendor product and ensure that the imported content is not available for execution.

SCAP.R.500: The product SHALL be able to select a specific SCAP source data stream when processing an SCAP data stream collection.

    SCAP Capability: ☑ ACS   ☐ CVE   ☐ OCIL

    Required Vendor Information:

    SCAP.V.500.1: The vendor SHALL provide documentation and instruction on how to select a specific data stream (by ID) when processing an SCAP data stream collection.

Required Test Procedures:

SCAP.T.500.1: The tester SHALL validate that the vendor product can selectively choose and apply a specific, valid SCAP data stream.

SCAP.R.600: The product SHALL be able to select a specific XCCDF benchmark within an SCAP source data stream or data stream collection when multiple XCCDF benchmarks are present.

    SCAP Capability: ☑ ACS   ☐ CVE   ☐ OCIL

Required Vendor Information:

SCAP.V.600.1: The vendor SHALL provide documentation and instruction on how to select a specific XCCDF benchmark (by ID) when processing an SCAP data stream or data stream collection with multiple benchmarks.

Required Test Procedures:

SCAP.T.600.1: The tester SHALL validate that the vendor product can selectively choose and apply a specific, valid XCCDF benchmark.

SCAP.R.700: The product SHALL be able to select a specific XCCDF profile within an SCAP source data stream or data stream collection when multiple XCCDF profiles are present.

    SCAP Capability: ☑ ACS   ☐ CVE   ☐ OCIL

Required Vendor Information:

SCAP.V.700.1: The vendor SHALL provide documentation and instruction on how to select a specific XCCDF profile (by ID) when processing an SCAP data stream or data stream collection.

Required Test Procedures:

SCAP.T.700.1: The tester SHALL validate that the vendor product can selectively choose and apply a specific valid XCCDF profile.

SCAP.R.800: The product SHALL enable the user to import signed and unsigned SCAP source data streams.

    SCAP Capability: ☑ ACS   ☐ CVE   ☐ OCIL

Required Vendor Information:

SCAP.V.800.1: The vendor SHALL provide documentation explaining how an SCAP source data stream can be imported into the product and subsequently executed.

Required Test Procedures:

SCAP.T.800.1: The tester SHALL verify that the product documentation includes instructions on how the end user can import an SCAP source data stream.

SCAP.T.800.2: The tester SHALL import a valid unsigned SCAP source data stream into the vendor product and ensure that the imported content is available for execution.

SCAP.T.800.3: The tester SHALL import a valid signed SCAP source data stream into the vendor product and ensure that the imported content is available for execution.

SCAP.R.900: The product SHALL be able to validate digitally signed SCAP source data streams and MAY reject source content that has an invalid signature.

SCAP Capability: ☑ ACS ☐ CVE ☐ OCIL

Required Vendor Information:

SCAP.V.900.1: The vendor SHALL provide documentation explaining how validation of digital signature validation is performed and where errors from validation will be displayed within the product output.

Required Test Procedures:

SCAP.T.900.1: The tester SHALL verify that the product documentation includes instructions on how the digital signature is validated.

SCAP.T.900.2: The tester SHALL verify that the vendor product can correctly validate the digital signature of a source data stream.

SCAP.T.900.3: The tester SHALL verify that the vendor product correctly identifies and reports an error when processing a data stream with an invalid digital signature.

SCAP.R.1000: The product SHALL recognize and reject SCAP source data streams that have signatures based on invalid certificates.

This requirement has been deferred.

SCAP.R.1100: The product SHALL be able to correctly import all earlier versions of SCAP content supported by [NIST SP 800-126 R3][15].

SCAP Capability: ☑ ACS ☐ CVE ☐ OCIL

Required Vendor Information:

SCAP.V.1100.1: The vendor SHALL provide documentation explaining how earlier versions of SCAP content can be imported into the product and subsequently executed.

Required Test Procedures:

SCAP.T.1100.1: Using the vendor product, the tester SHALL execute a valid SCAP source data stream based on SCAP 1.1 and SCAP 1.2 content.

SCAP.R.1200: The product SHALL be able to determine the applicability of an imported SCAP source data stream by evaluating the associated OVAL definition for the CPE Name on an XCCDF

---

[15] The products supporting SCAP 1.3 SHALL be capable of processing the legacy SCAP 1.2 and 1.1 content versions.

\<Benchmark\>, \<Profile\>, \<Group\>, or \<Rule\> and verifying that the associated XCCDF content applies to the target system.

    SCAP Capability: ☑ ACS   ☐ CVE   ☐ OCIL

    Required Vendor Information:

    SCAP.V.1200.1: The vendor SHALL provide instructions on how the product indicates the applicability of the imported SCAP source data stream to a target platform. Instructions SHOULD also describe how the imported data stream is indicated to not be applicable for a target platform. This requirement is testing the use of the OVAL check associated with a CPE name via the CPE dictionary and platform ID to determine applicability of the data stream.

    Required Test Procedures:

    SCAP.T.1200.1: The tester SHALL import an SCAP source data stream into the product that contains a CPE Name and platform ID and related OVAL definition not applicable for the target system. The tester SHALL verify that the product declines to execute the non-applicable tests.

    SCAP.T.1200.2: The tester SHALL import an SCAP source data stream into the product that contains a CPE Name and platform ID and related OVAL definition applicable for the target system. The tester SHALL verify that the product executes the applicable tests.

SCAP.R.1300: The product SHALL report and MAY reject SCAP source data stream collection content that is invalid according to the SCAP source data stream and\or its component XML schemas and Schematron schemas.[16]

    SCAP Capability: ☑ ACS   ☐ CVE   ☐ OCIL

    Required Vendor Information:

    SCAP.V.1300.1: The vendor SHALL provide instructions on how validation of SCAP source data stream collection content is performed and where errors from validation will be displayed within the product output.

    Required Test Procedures:

    SCAP.T.1300.1: The tester SHALL attempt to import known-invalid SCAP source data stream collection content into the vendor product and examine the product output to validate that the product reports the invalid SCAP source data stream collection content. The product MAY reject the content as invalid according to the SCAP source data stream collection schema and Schematron schemas.

    SCAP.T.1300.2: The tester SHALL attempt to import known-invalid XCCDF component content into the vendor product and examine the product output to validate that the product reports the invalid XCCDF content. The product MAY reject the content as invalid according to the XCCDF XML schema and Schematron schema.

---

[16]   This does not imply that the product being tested MUST use Schematron; the product needs only to produce the same results as the Schematron implementation.

SCAP.T.1300.3: The tester SHALL attempt to import known-invalid OVAL component content that is part of an SCAP source data stream into the vendor product and examine the product output to validate that the product reports the invalid OVAL content. The product MAY reject the content as invalid according to the OVAL Definition schema and Schematron schemas.

SCAP.T.1300.4: The tester SHALL attempt to import known-invalid CPE dictionary component content into the vendor product and examine the product output to validate that the product reports the invalid CPE dictionary content. The product MAY reject the content as invalid according to the CPE dictionary XML schema.

SCAP.R.1400: The product SHALL report and MAY reject SCAP source data stream collection content that includes an OCIL component that is invalid according to the OCIL XML schema.

SCAP Capability: ☐ ACS   ☐ CVE   ☑ OCIL

Required Vendor Information:

SCAP.V.1400.1: The vendor SHALL provide instructions on how validation of SCAP source data stream collection that includes an invalid OCIL component is performed and where errors from validation will be displayed within the product output.

Required Test Procedures:

SCAP.T.1400.1: The tester SHALL attempt to import an SCAP source data stream collection that includes an invalid OCIL component content into the vendor product and examine the product output to validate that the product reports the invalid OCIL content. The product MAY reject the content as invalid according to the OCIL XML schema.

SCAP.R.1500: The product SHALL be able to correctly process USGCB source data streams as input and produce valid results. If there are no USGCB source data streams for the platform(s) being tested, then this requirement is not applicable.

SCAP Capability: ☑ ACS   ☐ CVE   ☐ OCIL

Required Vendor Information:

SCAP.V.1500.1: The vendor SHALL provide instructions on how to import and execute valid USGCB source data streams.

SCAP.V.1500.2: The lab or the vendor SHALL provide the scan results for each tested platform using USGCB content associated with the platforms for which validation is being sought.

Required Test Procedures:

All the applicable USGCB source data streams published to https://usgcb.nist.gov/[17] SHALL be used for testing this requirement.

SCAP.T.1500.1: The lab or the vendor SHALL evaluate the target platforms in a managed configuration for Windows and standalone configuration for other platforms (i.e., RHEL, Mac

---

[17] According to NIST Special Publication 800-70 Revision 4, the final USGCB data streams are published to https://usgcb.nist.gov.

OS, Unix, etc.), and produce results. If the testing is performed by the vendor, the source data streams, the scan results, and their hashes[18] will be submitted to the lab for verification.

SCAP.T.1500.2: The tester SHALL review the scan results to ensure the files pass the SCAPVal validation without any errors.

SCAP.R.1510: The product SHALL be able to correctly evaluate a patches up-to-date XCCDF rule which references an OVAL source data stream component consistent with the normative guidance specified in [NIST SP 800-126 R3], against target systems of the target platform type and produce the expected results.

> **SCAP Capability:** ☑ ACS ☐ CVE ☐ OCIL

> **Required Vendor Information:**

> SCAP.V.1510.1: The vendor SHALL provide instructions on how to import and execute a valid SCAP source data stream with a patches up-to-date XCCDF rule. The vendor SHALL also provide instructions on where the resultant ARF XML Result output can be viewed by the tester.

> **Required Test Procedures:**

> Per vendor instruction in SCAP.V.1510, the tester SHALL evaluate the target platform(s) using test content with patches up-to-date XCCDF rule implemented via numerous and single OVAL patch class definitions, validate results produced with SCAPVal, and compare actual results to expected results, ensuring actual results match expected results.

> SCAP.T.1510.1: The tester SHALL evaluate the target platform(s) using a source data stream with an XCCDF patches up-to-date rule implemented via numerous OVAL patch class definitions in a domain connected configuration[19] for Windows and standalone configuration for other platforms, validate results produced with SCAPVal, and compare the scan results produced by the product to the expected results, ensuring the actual results match the expected results.

> SCAP.T.1510.2: The tester SHALL evaluate the target platform(s) using a source data stream with an XCCDF patches up-to-date rule implemented via a single OVAL patch class definition, in a domain connected configuration for Windows and standalone configuration for other platforms, validate results produced with SCAPVal, and compare the scan results produced by the product to the expected results, ensuring the actual results match the expected results.

SCAP.R.1600: If the product requires a specific configuration of the target platform that is not in compliance with the USGCB checklist, the vendor SHALL provide documentation indicating which settings require modification and a rationale for each changed setting. Products SHOULD only require changes to the target platform if needed for product functionality.

> **NOTE:** Pursuant to the U.S. Office of Management and Budget (OMB) Memorandum M-08-22 to Federal CIOs: "Both industry and government information technology providers must use SCAP validated tools with FDCC Scanner capability to certify their products operate correctly with FDCC configurations and do not alter FDCC settings." [OMB M-08-22] Products

---

[18] The hashes SHALL comply with *Annex A: Approved Security Functions* of [FIPS 140-2].
[19] "Domain connected configuration" is when a Windows platform is joined to an Active Directory domain.

undergoing SCAP validations are required by OMB to make this self-assertion. Listing non-complaint settings in no way negates the OMB M-08-22 requirement.

SCAP Capability: ☑ ACS   ☐ CVE   ☐ OCIL

Required Vendor Information:

SCAP.V.1600.1: The vendor SHALL provide an English language document to the lab that indicates which settings require modification and a rationale for each changed setting. This content will be used on NIST web pages to explain details about each validated product and thus SHOULD contain only information that is to be publicly released.

Required Test Procedures:

SCAP.T.1600.1: The tester SHALL review the provided documentation to ensure that each indicated setting includes an associated rationale.

SCAP.R.1700: The product SHALL be able to correctly process the test content that is representative of SCAP expressed content published at NIST National Checklist Program Repository, and the OVAL repository[20] which is associated with the platforms for which validation is being sought.

SCAP Capability: ☑ ACS   ☐ CVE   ☐ OCIL

Required Vendor Information:

SCAP.V.1700.1: The vendor SHALL provide instructions on how to execute a previously imported valid data stream for platforms supported.

Required Test Procedures:

SCAP.T.1700.1: Per vendor instruction in SCAP.V.1700, the tester SHALL evaluate a target platform using the test content that is representative of NIST NCP and OVAL repository, validate results produced with SCAPVal tool, and ensure actual results match expected results.

SCAP.R.1800: The product SHALL be able to determine the applicability of an imported SCAP source data stream by evaluating the associated OCIL questionnaire for the CPE Name and platform ID on an XCCDF <Benchmark>, <Profile>, <Group>, or <Rule> and verifying that the associated XCCDF content applies to the target system.

SCAP Capability: ☐ ACS   ☐ CVE   ☑ OCIL

Required Vendor Information:

SCAP.V.1800.1: The vendor SHALL provide instructions on how the product indicates the applicability of the imported SCAP source data stream to a target platform. Instructions SHOULD also describe how the product indicates data streams are not applicable for a target platform. This requirement is testing the use of the OCIL questionnaire associated with a CPE name via the CPE dictionary and the platform id to determine applicability of the data stream.

---

[20] The OVAL repository is hosted by Center for Internet Security: https://oval.cisecurity.org/repository.

Required Test Procedures:

SCAP.T.1800.1: The tester SHALL import an SCAP source data stream into the product that contains a CPE Name and related OCIL questionnaire not applicable for the target system. The tester SHALL verify that the product declines to execute the non-applicable tests.

SCAP.R.1900: The product SHALL be able to correctly evaluate a valid OVAL Definition file and external variable file, where the contents of the OVAL Definition file are consistent with the normative guidance[21] specified in [NIST SP 800-126 R1], against target systems of the target platform type and produce a result for each definition using the OVAL XML Full Results expressed as Single Machine Without System Characteristics, Single Machine With System Characteristics, and Single Machine With Thin Results.[22]

> **SCAP Capability:** ☑ ACS ☐ CVE ☐ OCIL

Required Vendor Information:

SCAP.V.1900.1: The vendor SHALL provide instructions on how a valid OVAL Definitions file and external variable file can be imported into the product for interpretation. The vendor SHALL also provide instructions on where the resultant OVAL XML Results output can be viewed by the tester.

Required Test Procedure

SCAP.T.1900.1: The tester SHALL run the product using valid OVAL Definitions files and an external variable file against the test system of the target platform type. The actual results SHALL match the expected results.

SCAP.T.1900.2: The tester SHALL validate the resulting OVAL XML Full Results by importing the result set into the SCAPVal utility and checking for validation errors.

SCAP.T.1900.3: The tester SHALL validate that the resulting OVAL XML Full Results are available for viewing by the user.

SCAP.T.1900.4: After the test system is assessed using the OVAL file, the tester SHALL capture the successful results of the scan and verify the correctness of the results.

SCAP.T.1900.5: When the OVAL Definition file has been evaluated with the external variable file that defines different values for the variables, the tester SHALL validate that the OVAL XML Full Results file includes unique variable values as defined in the external variables file.

SCAP.R.2000: The product SHALL be able to correctly evaluate a valid OVAL Definition component that is part of an SCAP source data stream, where the contents of the OVAL definition file are consistent with the normative guidance[23] specified in [NIST SP 800-126 R3] and [NIST SP 800-126A], against target systems of the target platform type and produce a result for each definition using the OVAL XML Full Results expressed as Single Machine Without System

---

[21] The supported OVAL tests are published at https://csrc.nist.gov/projects/scap-validation-program.
[22] The use case for OVAL-Only Scanning is described in Section 5.4 of [NIST SP 800-126 R1].
[23] The supported OVAL tests are published at https://csrc.nist.gov/projects/scap-validation-program.

Characteristics, Single Machine With System Characteristics, and Single Machine With Thin Results.

SCAP Capability: ☑ ACS   ☐ CVE   ☐ OCIL

Required Vendor Information:

SCAP.V.2000.1: The vendor SHALL provide instructions on how a valid SCAP data stream file can be imported into the product for interpretation. The vendor SHALL also provide instructions on where the resultant SCAP Results output can be viewed by the tester.

Required Test Procedure:

SCAP.T.2000.1: The tester SHALL run the product using a valid SCAP data stream against the target systems of the target platform type. The actual results SHALL match the expected results.

SCAP.T.2000.2: The tester SHALL validate the resulting SCAP data stream by importing it into the SCAPVal utility and checking for any validation errors.

SCAP.T.2000.3: The tester SHALL validate that the resulting SCAP data stream is available for viewing by the user.

SCAP.T.2000.4: The tester SHALL capture the successful results of the import and verify the correctness of the results.

SCAP.R.2100: The product SHALL be able to correctly evaluate a valid OCIL Questionnaire file against test systems of the target platform type, and produce a valid OCIL Output file (i.e., file that includes both the original content and the evaluation results) using the format defined by the OCIL XML schema.

SCAP Capability: ☐ ACS   ☐ CVE   ☑ OCIL

Required Vendor Information:

SCAP.V.2100.1: The vendor SHALL provide instructions on how a valid OCIL Questionnaire file can be imported into the product for interpretation. The vendor SHALL also provide instructions on where the resultant OCIL Output file can be viewed by the tester.

Required Test Procedure:

SCAP.T.2100.1: The tester SHALL run the product using valid OCIL document files against the test systems of the target platform type. The results SHALL be verified by the tester, ensuring each OCIL definition and criteria contained within the definition produces the correct response.

SCAP.T.2100.2: The tester SHALL validate the resulting OCIL Output file with the SCAPVal utility and check for any validation errors.

SCAP.T.2100.3: The tester SHALL validate that the resulting OCIL Output file is available for viewing by the user.

SCAP.R.2200: The product SHALL be able to correctly evaluate a valid OCIL Questionnaire component that is part of an SCAP source data stream against target systems of the target platform

type, and produce a valid OCIL results component (i.e., component that includes both the original content and the evaluation results) using the format defined by the OCIL XML schema.

SCAP Capability: ☐ ACS   ☐ CVE   ☑ OCIL

Required Vendor Information:

SCAP.V.2200.1: The vendor SHALL provide instructions on how a valid OCIL Questionnaire file that is part of an SCAP source data stream can be imported into the product for interpretation. The vendor SHALL also provide instructions on where the resultant SCAP data stream can be viewed by the tester.

Required Test Procedure:

SCAP.T.2200.1: The tester SHALL run the product using valid SCAP data stream files against the target systems of the target platform type. The actual results SHALL match the expected results.

SCAP.T.2200.2: The tester SHALL validate the resulting SCAP data stream by importing it into the SCAPVal utility and checking for any validation errors.

SCAP.T.2200.3: The tester SHALL validate that the resulting SCAP data stream is available for viewing by the user.

SCAP.R.2300: **The product SHALL indicate the correct CCE ID for each configuration issue referenced within the product that has an associated CCE ID (i.e., the product's CCE mapping MUST be correct).**

SCAP Capability: ☑ ACS   ☐ CVE   ☐ OCIL

Required Vendor Information:

SCAP.V.2300.1: None.

Required Test Procedures:

SCAP.T.2300.1: Using the product output from SCAP.R.2930, the tester SHALL compare the vendor data against the official CCE description. The tester SHALL perform the comparison using a non-vendor-directed sample comprised of greater than or equal to 10 and less than or equal to 30 of the total configuration issue items with CCE IDs. The tester SHOULD prove that the vendor's CCE ID correctly maps to the configuration issue. This test ensures that the product correctly maps to CCE IDs, but does not test for completeness of the mapping.

SCAP.R.2400: **The product SHALL associate an existing CCE ID to each configuration issue referenced within the product for which a CCE ID exists (i.e., the product's CCE mapping MUST be complete).**

SCAP Capability: ☑ ACS   ☐ CVE   ☐ OCIL

Required Vendor Information:

SCAP.V.2400.1: None.

Required Test Procedures:

SCAP.T.2400.1: Using the list of configuration issue items produced in SCAP.R.2930, the tester SHALL examine the descriptions and search the CCE dictionary for corresponding CCE IDs. The tester SHALL perform this using a non-vendor-directed sample comprised of 10 % of the total configuration issue items with no CCE IDs, up to a maximum of 30. The tester does not need to rigorously prove that no CCE ID exists, only that there does not appear to be a match. This test ensures that the product has a complete mapping to CCE, but does not test the correctness of the mapped data.

SCAP.R.2500: If the product natively contains a product dictionary (as opposed to dynamically importing content containing CPE names), the product MUST contain CPE naming data from the current official CPE Dictionary.

> **NOTE:** This requirement does not apply if the product is using the official dynamic CPE Dictionary as provided on the NVD web site or as part of an SCAP source data stream.

SCAP Capability: ☑ ACS ☐ CVE ☐ OCIL

Required Vendor Information:

SCAP.V.2500.1: The vendor SHALL provide a list of all CPE names included in the product using the standard CPE Dictionary XML schema as provided in the CPE Specification version cited in Section 2.

SCAP.V.2500.2: If the vendor product includes CPE names that are not in the official CPE Dictionary, a listing of exceptions MUST be provided.

Required Test Procedures:

SCAP.T.2500.1: The tester SHALL compare the vendor-provided list of CPE Names against the official CPE Dictionary.[24] The tester SHALL verify that all exceptions found match the list of exceptions provided by the vendor.

SCAP.R.2600: Products MUST process CPEs referenced in an *<xccdf:platform>* element directly or by a *<cpe2:fact-ref>* contained within a referenced *<cpe2:platform-specification>* element as specified in [NIST SP 800-126 R3].

SCAP Capability: ☑ ACS ☐ CVE ☐ OCIL

Required Vendor Information:

SCAP.V.2600.1: The vendor SHALL provide instructions describing how to import an SCAP source data stream that contains references to CPEs in an *<xccdf:platform>* element directly or by a *<cpe2:fact-ref>* contained within a referenced *<cpe2:platform-specification>* element and have it applied against a known platform. The vendor SHALL also provide instructions on how to view the results of the application of the content against the platform.

Required Test Procedures:

---

[24] Official Common Platform Enumeration (CPE) Dictionary is available at https://nvd.nist.gov/products/cpe.

SCAP.T.2600.1: The tester SHALL import the known content into the product and apply it against a known platform.

SCAP.T.2600.2: The tester SHALL import the results of the content into the SCAPVal utility and check for any validation errors.

SCAP.T.2600.3: The tester SHALL ensure the actual results match the expected results that are provided by the SCAP Validation Program.

SCAP.R.2700: The product SHALL indicate the correct CVE ID or metadata for each software flaw and/or patch definition referenced within the product that has an associated CVE ID (i.e., the product's CVE mapping MUST be correct).

       SCAP Capability: ☐ ACS   ☑ CVE   ☐ OCIL

       Required Vendor Information:

       SCAP.V.2700.1: None

       Required Test Procedures:

       SCAP.T.2700.1: Using the product output from SCAP.R.2920, the tester SHALL compare the vendor data against the official NVD CVE ID description and references. The tester SHALL perform this test using a non-vendor-directed sample comprised of 10 % of the total software flaws and/or patches with CVE IDs, up to a maximum of 30. The tester does not need to rigorously prove that the vendor's software flaw and/or patch description matches the NVD CVE description, but merely needs to identify that the two descriptions appear to pertain to the same vulnerability. This test ensures that the product correctly maps to CVE, but does not test for completeness of the mapping.

       It is sufficient to provide specific URLs that link to the NVD website. For example, "https://nvd.nist.gov/vuln/detail/CVE-2017-7269". It is not sufficient to provide a generic URL to https://nvd.nist.gov/vuln.

SCAP.R.2800: The product SHALL associate an existing CVE ID to each software flaw and/or patch referenced within the product for which a CVE ID exists (i.e., the product's CVE mapping MUST be complete).

       SCAP Capability: ☐ ACS   ☑ CVE   ☐ OCIL

       Required Vendor Information:

       SCAP.V.2800.1: None.

       Required Test Procedures:

       SCAP.T.2800.1: Using the list of software flaws produced in SCAP.R.2920, the tester SHALL examine the descriptions and search the NVD for corresponding CVE IDs. The tester SHALL perform this using a non-vendor-directed sample comprised of 10 % of the total software flaws and/or patches with no CVE IDs, up to a maximum of 30. The tester does not need to rigorously prove that no CVE ID exists, only that there does not appear to be a match. This test ensures that the product has a complete mapping to CVE, but does not test the correctness of the mapped data.

SCAP.R.2850: The product SHALL be able to identify SWID tags installed on a target asset using OVAL inventory class definitions that are part of an SCAP source data stream. The product SHALL use the methods described in [NIST SP 800-126 R3][25].

SCAP Capability: ☑ ACS ☐ CVE ☐ OCIL

Required Vendor Information:

SCAP.V.2850.1: The vendor SHALL provide instructions on how the product identifies SWID tags using OVAL inventory class definitions that are part of an SCAP source data stream.

Required Test Procedures:

SCAP.T.2850.1: The tester SHALL import the SCAP 1.3 source data stream, apply it to a known target, and produce an SCAP result data stream conforming to the ARF specification.

SCAP.T.2850.2: The tester SHALL validate the results produced using SCAPVal; the validation MUST NOT produce any errors.

SCAP.T.2850.3: The tester SHALL compare the actual results to the expected results ensuring the results match.

SCAP.R.2860: The product SHALL be able to identify SWID tags installed on a target asset using OVAL inventory class definitions that are part of a standalone OVAL Definition file. The product SHALL use the methods described in [NIST SP 800-126 R3][26].

SCAP Capability: ☑ ACS ☐ CVE ☐ OCIL

Required Vendor Information:

SCAP.V.2860.1: The vendor SHALL provide instructions on how the product identifies SWID tags using OVAL inventory class definitions that are part of a standalone OVAL Definition file.

Required Test Procedures:

SCAP.T.2860.1: The tester SHALL import OVAL inventory class definitions that are part of a standalone OVAL Definition file, apply it to a known target, and produce an OVAL results file conforming to the OVAL specification.

SCAP.T.2860.2: The tester SHALL validate the results produced using SCAPVal; the validation MUST NOT produce any errors.

SCAP.T.2860.3: The tester SHALL compare the actual results to the expected results ensuring the results match.

---

[25] See Section 3.6 Software Identification (SWID) Tags of the [NIST SP 800-126 R3].
[26] *Ibid.*

4.3 SCAP Result(s) Data Stream

This section addresses those requirements that assess a product's ability to produce validated SCAP results.

SCAP.R.2900: SCAP result data streams SHALL be produced by the product in compliance with the SCAP result data streams as specified in [NIST SP 800-126 R3] **and** [NIST SP 800-126A]**.**

SCAP Capability: ☑ ACS   ☐ CVE   ☐ OCIL

Required Vendor Information:

SCAP.V.2900.1: The vendor SHALL provide instruction on where the corresponding SCAP result data stream file(s) can be located for inspection.

Required Test Procedures:

SCAP.T.2900.1: The tester SHALL visually inspect SCAP results to verify that the ARF report contains a report object for each XCCDF, OVAL, and OCIL component executed when a source data stream is evaluated against a target. Each component result SHALL be captured as a separate <arf:report> element[27] in the <arf:asset-report-collection> element.

SCAP.T.2900.2: The tester SHALL validate the SCAP result data stream files with SCAPVal and verify the result data stream passes without errors.

SCAP.R.2910: The product SHALL be able to correctly import and evaluate SCAP source data streams which reference external content consistent with the normative guidance specified in [NIST SP 800-126 R3]**, against target systems of the target platform type and produce the expected results.**

SCAP Capability: ☑ ACS   ☐ CVE   ☐ OCIL

Required Vendor Information:

SCAP.V.2910.1: The vendor SHALL provide instructions on how to import and execute a valid SCAP source data stream with references to external content. The vendor SHALL also provide instructions on where the resultant ARF XML Result output can be viewed by the tester.

Required Test Procedures:

Per vendor instruction in SCAP.V.2910, the tester SHALL evaluate the target platform(s) using test content with references to external content, validate results produced with SCAPVal, and compare actual results to expected results, ensuring actual results match expected results.

SCAP.T.2910.1: The tester SHALL evaluate the target platform(s), in a domain connected configuration for Windows and standalone configuration for other platforms, validate results produced with SCAPVal, and compare the scan results produced by the product to the expected results, ensuring the actual results match the expected results.

---

[27] For instance, if a source data stream which includes four components (XCCDF, OVAL, CPE-Dictionary, and CPE-OVAL) is evaluated, then the ARF report SHALL include three component results (XCCDF results, OVAL results, CPE-OVAL results).

SCAP.R.2920: The product SHALL be able to assign CVE identifiers to rule results in compliance with the SCAP result data streams as specified in NIST SP 800-126 R3].

    SCAP Capability: ☑ ACS   ☑ CVE   ☐ OCIL

    Required Vendor Information:

    SCAP.V.2920.1: The vendor SHALL provide instruction on where the SCAP Result Data Stream files can be located for inspection.

    Required Test Procedures:

    SCAP.T.2920.1: The tester SHALL visually inspect the results to verify that the CVE identifiers are included within the <xccdf:rule-result> element. The SCAP Result Data Streams MUST be processed by the SCAPVal utility without any errors.

SCAP.R.2930: The product SHALL be able to assign CCE identifiers to rule results in compliance with the SCAP result data streams as specified in [NIST SP 800-126 R3].

    SCAP Capability: ☑ ACS   ☐ CVE   ☐ OCIL

    Required Vendor Information:

    SCAP.V.2930.1: The vendor SHALL provide instruction on where the SCAP Result Data Stream files can be located for inspection.

    Required Test Procedures:

    SCAP.T.2930.1: The tester SHALL visually inspect the results to verify that the CCE identifiers are included within the <xccdf:rule-result> element. The SCAP Result Data Streams MUST be processed by the SCAPVal utility without any errors.

SCAP.R.2940: The product SHALL be able to assign CPE identifiers to rule results in compliance with the SCAP result data streams as specified in [NIST SP 800-126 R3]].

    SCAP Capability: ☑ ACS   ☐ CVE   ☐ OCIL

    Required Vendor Information:

    SCAP.V.2940.1: The vendor SHALL provide instruction on where the SCAP Result Data Stream files can be located for inspection.

    Required Test Procedures:

    SCAP.T.2940.1: The tester SHALL visually inspect the results to verify that the CPE identifiers are included within the <xccdf:rule-result> element. The SCAP Result Data Streams MUST be processed by the SCAPVal utility without any errors.

SCAP.R.3000: The product SHALL be able to process XCCDF components that are part of an SCAP source data stream and generate XCCDF component results within an SCAP result data stream in accordance with the XCCDF specification for the target platform.[28]

      SCAP Capability: ☑ ACS   ☐ CVE   ☐ OCIL

      NOTE: "XCCDF components" refer to the elements such as benchmark, profile, group, rule, value, and test result.

      Required Vendor Information:

      SCAP.V.3000.1: The vendor SHALL provide instructions on how to import XCCDF component content that is part of SCAP source data streams for execution and provide instructions on where the XCCDF component results can be located for visual inspection. The purpose of this requirement is to ensure that the product produces valid XCCDF Results and a matching "pass", "fail", "error", "unknown", "notapplicable", "notchecked", "notselected", "informational", or "fixed" result for a given rule.

      Required Test Procedures:

      SCAP.T.3000.1: The tester SHALL import a known valid XCCDF component content that is part of SCAP data streams for the target platform into the vendor product and execute it according to the product operation instructions provided by the vendor. The tester will inspect the product output ensuring XCCDF components are compliant with the XCCDF specification.

      SCAP.T.3000.2: The tester SHALL validate the resulting XCCDF component results within an SCAP result data stream output using the SCAPVal utility. This validation MUST NOT produce any validation errors.

      SCAP.T.3000.3: The tester SHALL compare the product results to the expected results ensuring that the "pass", "fail", "error", "unknown", "notapplicable", "notchecked", "notselected", "informational", or "fixed" results match for each <xccdf:Rule>.

SCAP.R.3005: The product SHALL be able to process XCCDF Tailoring component (<xccdf:Tailoring>) that is part of an SCAP source data stream as well as XCCDF Tailoring component that is external to the source datastream and generate XCCDF component results within an SCAP result data stream in accordance with the XCCDF specification for the target platform.

      SCAP Capability: ☑ ACS   ☐ CVE   ☐ OCIL

      Required Vendor Information:

      SCAP.V.3005.1: The vendor SHALL provide instructions on how to import XCCDF Tailoring component content that is part of or external to the SCAP source data streams for execution and provide instructions on where the XCCDF component results can be located for visual inspection. The purpose of this requirement is to ensure that the product produces valid XCCDF Results and the results match the expected results for all given rules.

---

[28] XCCDF Specification in [NISTIR 7275 R4].

Required Test Procedures:

SCAP.T.3005.1: The tester SHALL import a known valid XCCDF Tailoring component content that is part of SCAP source data streams for the target platform into the vendor product and execute it according to the product operation instructions provided by the vendor. The tester will inspect the product output ensuring XCCDF components are compliant with the XCCDF specification.

SCAP.T.3005.2: The tester SHALL import a known valid XCCDF Tailoring component content that is external to the SCAP source data streams for the target platform into the vendor product and execute it according to the product operation instructions provided by the vendor. The tester will inspect the product output ensuring XCCDF components are compliant with the XCCDF specification.

SCAP.T.3005.3: The tester SHALL validate the resulting XCCDF component results within an SCAP result data stream output using the SCAPVal utility. This validation MUST NOT produce any validation errors.

SCAP.T.3005.4: The tester SHALL compare the product results to the expected results ensuring that all the results match the expected results.

SCAP.R.3010: The product SHALL be able to select and process XCCDF Benchmark components, which do not include <xccdf:Profile> elements, that are part of an SCAP source data stream and generate XCCDF component results within an SCAP result data stream in accordance with the XCCDF specification for the target platform.

SCAP Capability: ☑ ACS   ☐ CVE   ☐ OCIL

Required Vendor Information:

SCAP.V.3010.1: The vendor SHALL provide instructions on how to import XCCDF component content without <xccdf:Profile> elements that is part of SCAP source data streams for execution and provide instructions on where the XCCDF component results can be located for visual inspection. The purpose of this requirement is to ensure that the product produces valid XCCDF Results and the results match the expected results for all given rules.

Required Test Procedures:

SCAP.T.3010.1: The tester SHALL import a known valid XCCDF component content without <xccdf:Profile> elements that is part of SCAP data streams for the target platform into the vendor product and execute it according to the product operation instructions provided by the vendor. The tester will inspect the product output ensuring XCCDF components are compliant with the XCCDF specification.

SCAP.T.3010.2: The tester SHALL validate the resulting XCCDF component results within an SCAP result data stream output using the SCAPVal utility. This validation MUST NOT produce any validation errors.

SCAP.T.3010.3: The tester SHALL compare the product results to the expected results ensuring that all the results match the expected results.

SCAP.R.3100: For all CCE IDs in the SCAP source data stream, the product SHALL correctly display the CCE ID with its associated XCCDF Rule in the product output.

SCAP Capability: ☑ ACS ☐ CVE ☐ OCIL

Required Vendor Information:

SCAP.V.3100.1: The vendor SHALL provide instructions on where the XCCDF Rules and their associated CCE IDs can be visually inspected within the product output.

Required Test Procedures:

SCAP.T.3100.1: The tester SHALL visually inspect a non-vendor-directed sample of 10 % of the XCCDF Rules, up to a maximum of 30, within the product output and reports to validate that the CCE IDs for each inspected XCCDF Rule match those found in the XCCDF source file.

SCAP.R.3200: The product output SHALL enable users to view the XML OCIL Questionnaires being consumed by the product (e.g., within the product user interface or through an XML dump of the OCIL questionnaires to a file).

SCAP Capability: ☐ ACS ☐ CVE ☑ OCIL

Required Vendor Information:

SCAP.V.3200.1: The vendor SHALL provide instructions on how the user can view the XML OCIL Questionnaires being consumed by the product.

Required Test Procedure:

SCAP.T.3200.1: The tester SHALL follow the provided vendor instructions to view the XML OCIL Questionnaires being consumed by the product and verify that access is provided as stated.

SCAP.R.3300: The product SHALL be able to produce "notchecked" results for unsupported checking systems. [29]

SCAP Capability: ☑ ACS ☐ CVE ☐ OCIL

Required Vendor Information:

SCAP.V.3300.1: The vendor SHALL provide instructions indicating how content for unsupported checking systems is processed.

Required Test Procedures:

SCAP.T.3300.1: The tester SHALL import a valid SCAP source data stream containing a check system unsupported by the vendor product for the target platform into the product and execute the data stream according to the product operation instructions provided by the vendor. The tester

---

[29] XCCDF Specification in [NISTIR 7275 R4].

SHALL inspect the product output to validate that it includes "notchecked" results for the unsupported checking system.

SCAP.R.3400: The product output in ARF format SHALL enable users to view the SCAP source data stream collection that was used to generate the results against the target.

> **SCAP Capability:**   ☑ ACS   ☐ CVE   ☐ OCIL
>
> **Required Vendor Information:**
>
> SCAP.V.3400.1: The vendor SHALL provide instructions on how the user can view the ARF report produced by the product which includes the source content consumed by the product.
>
> **Required Test Procedure:**
>
> SCAP.T.3400.1: The tester SHALL follow the provided vendor instructions to view the ARF report and verify that the source data stream collection that was used to generate the results was included in the report as an <arf:report-request>.
>
> SCAP.T.3400.2: The tester SHALL import a valid SCAP source data stream with an <xccdf:Tailoring> component and execute the data stream according to the product operation instructions provided by the vendor. The tester SHALL inspect the product output to make sure the tailoring component was included in the ARF report as an <arf:report-request>.

SCAP.R.3500: For all SCAP source data streams, the product SHALL indicate the date the data was last generated and updated. The generated date is when the data was originally created/officially published. The updated date is the date the product obtained its copy of the data.

> **SCAP Capability:**   ☑ ACS   ☐ CVE   ☐ OCIL
>
> **Required Vendor Information:**
>
> SCAP.V.3500.1: The vendor SHALL provide instructions on where the dates for all imported SCAP source data streams can be inspected in the product output.
>
> **Required Test Procedures:**
>
> SCAP.T.3500.1: The tester SHALL visually inspect the product output for correctly recorded dates of all SCAP source data streams processed by the vendor product.

SCAP.R.3600: The product SHALL display the associated CCE ID for each configuration issue definition in the product output (i.e., the product displays CCE IDs).

> **SCAP Capability:**   ☑ ACS   ☐ CVE   ☐ OCIL
>
> **Required Vendor Information:**
>
> SCAP.V.3600.1: The vendor SHALL provide instructions on how product output can be generated that contains a listing of all security configuration issue items, with associated CCE IDs when available. Instructions SHALL include where the CCE IDs and the associated vendor supplied and/or official CCE descriptions can be located within the product output.

This publication is available free of charge from: https://doi.org/10.6028/NIST.IR.7511r5

Required Test Procedures:

SCAP.T.3600.1: The tester SHALL visually inspect, within the product output, a non-vendor-directed set of 30 security configuration issue items, to ensure that the CCE IDs are displayed. This test is not intended to determine whether the product correctly maps to CCE or whether it provides a complete mapping.

SCAP.R.3800: **A product's machine-readable output MUST provide the CPE naming data using CPE names.**

    SCAP Capability: ☑ ACS   ☐ CVE   ☐ OCIL

Required Vendor Information:

SCAP.V.3800.1: The vendor SHALL provide procedures and/or a test environment where machine-readable output containing the CPE naming data can be produced and inspected. The vendor SHALL provide a translation tool to create human-readable data for inspection if the provided output is not in a human-readable format (e.g., binary data, encrypted text).

Required Test Procedures:

SCAP.T.3800.1: The tester SHALL manually inspect the vendor-identified machine-readable output and ensure that CPE naming data is correct according to the CPE specification. The tester will do this by choosing a minimum of 30 vendor and product names in the product output that are also included in the official CPE Dictionary.

SCAP.R.3900: **The product SHALL allow users to locate configuration issue items using CCE IDs.**

    SCAP Capability: ☑ ACS   ☐ CVE   ☐ OCIL

Required Vendor Information:

SCAP.V.3900.1: The vendor SHALL provide documentation (printed or electronic) indicating how configuration issue items can be located using CCE IDs.

Required Test Procedures:

SCAP.T.3900.1: The tester SHALL verify that configuration issue items can be identified using CCE IDs. The tester SHALL perform this using a non-vendor-directed sample comprised of 10 % of the total configuration issue items, up to a maximum of 30.

SCAP.R.4000: **The product SHALL be able to correctly produce the Asset Identification Fields as specified in [NIST SP 800-126 R3] when assessing a target.**

    SCAP Capability: ☑ ACS   ☐ CVE   ☐ OCIL

Required Vendor Information:

SCAP.V.4000.1: The vendor SHALL provide documentation on how to import an SCAP data stream and how to apply it to a target system.

Required Test Procedures:

SCAP.T.4000.1: The tester SHALL import the SCAP source data stream and apply it to a known target, producing an SCAP result data stream.

SCAP.T.4000.2: The tester SHALL validate the results produced using SCAPVal; the validation MUST NOT produce any errors.

SCAP.T.4000.3: The tester SHALL visually inspect the results to ensure the Asset Identification Fields are as expected.

SCAP.R.4100: The product SHALL be able to correctly produce an SCAP result data stream conforming to the ARF specification for each XCCDF, OVAL, and OCIL component.

> **SCAP Capability:**   ☑ ACS   ☐ CVE   ☑ OCIL

Required Vendor Information:

SCAP.V.4100.1: The vendor SHALL supply documentation on how to import an SCAP data stream, apply it against a target, and produce an SCAP result data stream conforming to the ARF specification.

Required Test Procedures:

SCAP.T.4100.1: The tester SHALL import the SCAP 1.3 source data stream, apply it to a known target, and produce an SCAP result data stream conforming to the ARF specification.

SCAP.T.4100.2: The tester SHALL validate the results produced using SCAPVal; the validation MUST NOT produce any errors.

SCAP.T.4100.3: The tester SHALL compare the actual results to the expected results ensuring the results match.

SCAP.R.4200: The product SHALL provide a means to view the CVE Description and CVE references for each displayed CVE ID[30] within the product output.

> **SCAP Capability:**   ☐ ACS   ☑ CVE   ☐ OCIL

Required Vendor Information:

SCAP.V.4200.1: The vendor SHALL provide instructions on where the CVE IDs can be located within the product output. The vendor SHALL provide procedures and a test environment (if necessary) so that the product will output vulnerabilities with associated CVE IDs. Instructions SHALL include where the CVE IDs and the associated vendor-supplied and official CVE descriptions can be located within the product output. It is acceptable to have CVEs in the form of a specific link for each CVE to the NVD.

Required Test Procedures:

---

[30] This requirement can be met by providing a URL to the NVD CVE or MITRE CVE vulnerability summaries for the CVE IDs in question.

SCAP.T.4200.1: The tester SHALL select a non-vendor-directed sampling of CVE IDs from within the available forms of the product output. The tester SHALL determine that the product output enables the user to view, at minimum, the official CVE description and references.[31] The vendor MAY provide additional CVE descriptions and information. The tester SHALL perform this using a non-vendor-directed sample comprised of greater than or equal to 10 and less than or equal to 30 of the total CVE IDs available in the product output.

SCAP.R.4300: **For all static or product-bundled CCE data, the product SHALL indicate the date the data was last generated and updated. The generated date is when the data was originally created/officially published. The updated date is the date the product obtained its copy of the data.**

NOTE: This requirement is not applicable to the products that don't use static or product-bundled CCE data.

SCAP Capability: ☑ ACS ☐ CVE ☐ OCIL

Required Vendor Information:

SCAP.V.4300.1: The vendor SHALL provide instructions on where the dates for all offline CCE data can be inspected in the product output.

Required Test Procedures:

SCAP.T.4300.1: The tester SHALL visually inspect the product output for the dates of all static or bundled CCE data included with the vendor product.

SCAP.R.4400: **The product SHALL include the CVE ID(s) associated with each software flaw and/or patch definition in the product output (i.e., the product displays CVE IDs) where appropriate.[32]**

SCAP Capability: ☐ ACS ☑ CVE ☐ OCIL

Required Vendor Information:

SCAP.V.4400.1: The vendor SHALL provide instructions, and a test environment (if necessary), indicating how product output can be generated that contains a listing of all software flaws and patches with associated CVE IDs when available. CVE IDs SHOULD be used wherever possible. Instructions SHALL include where the CVE IDs and the associated vendor-supplied and/or official CVE descriptions can be located within the product output.

Required Test Procedures:

SCAP.T.4400.1: The tester SHALL visually inspect, within the product output, a non-vendor-selected sample comprised of greater than or equal to 10 and less than or equal to 30 of the total CVE IDs available in the product output to ensure that the CVE IDs are displayed. This test is not intended to determine whether the product correctly maps to CVE or whether it provides a complete mapping.

---

[31] The official CVE description and references are found at https://nvd.nist.gov/.
[32] In the case where the content being processed only requires results that do not contain CVE references this requirement does not apply.

SCAP.R.4500: If the product uses CVE, it SHALL include NVD CVSS base scores and vector strings for each CVE ID referenced in the product.

    SCAP Capability: ☐ ACS   ☑ CVE   ☐ OCIL

    Required Vendor Information:

    SCAP.V.4500.1: The vendor SHALL provide documentation explaining where the NVD CVSS base scores and vector strings can be located with the corresponding CVE ID.[33] The vendor MAY provide information about how the product can be updated with new NVD CVSS base scores and vector strings prior to testing.

    Required Test Procedure:

    SCAP.T.4500.1: The tester SHALL update the product's NVD base scores and vectors (using the vendor-provided update capability if it exists) and validate that the product displays the NVD CVSS base scores and vectors for 15 non-vendor-directed CVE IDs referenced in the product. The CVEs chosen MUST have an NVD vulnerability summary "last revision" date that is at least 30 days old. A link to the information on the NVD web site is sufficient for this test.

---

[33]   A link to the specific CVE entry on the NVD web site is sufficient for this test.

5.   Derived Test Requirements for Specific Capabilities

This section contains Derived Test Requirements for each of the defined SCAP capabilities. When a product is submitted for validation, the submitting organization will provide a list of SCAP capabilities the product possesses. The information regarding capabilities will be provided by the vendor as part of their submission package. To determine the correct test requirements for that product, the tester creates the union of all these capabilities using the chart below.

The matrix currently contains a total of three SCAP capabilities. As additional capabilities are available for validation, this list will be updated. Vendors seeking validation for an SCAP capability not listed should contact NIST at scap@nist.gov.

The following chart summarizes the requirements for each SCAP 1.3 capability.

Table 5-1. Required SCAP Components for Each SCAP Capability

Requirement ID	Authenticated Configuration Scanner (ACS)	CVE option	OCIL option
SCAP.R.100	X		
SCAP.R.200	X		
SCAP.R.300	X		
SCAP.R.400	X		
SCAP.R.500	X		
SCAP.R.600	X		
SCAP.R.700	X		
SCAP.R.800	X		
SCAP.R.900	X		
SCAP.R.1100	X		
SCAP.R.1200	X		
SCAP.R.1300	X		
SCAP.R.1400			X
SCAP.R.1500	X		
SCAP.R.1510	X		
SCAP.R.1600	X		
SCAP.R.1700	X		
SCAP.R.1800			X
SCAP.R.1900	X		
SCAP.R.2000	X		
SCAP.R.2100			X

Requirement ID	Authenticated Configuration Scanner (ACS)	CVE option	OCIL option
SCAP.R.2200			X
SCAP.R.2300	X		
SCAP.R.2400	X		
SCAP.R.2500	X		
SCAP.R.2600	X		
SCAP.R.2700		X	
SCAP.R.2800		X	
SCAP.R.2850	X		
SCAP.R.2860	X		
SCAP.R.2900	X		
SCAP.R.2910	X		
SCAP.R.2920	X	X	
SCAP.R.2930	X		
SCAP.R.2940	X		
SCAP.R.3000	X		
SCAP.R.3005	X		
SCAP.R.3010	X		
SCAP.R.3100	X		
SCAP.R.3200			X
SCAP.R.3300	X		
SCAP.R.3400	X		
SCAP.R.3500	X		
SCAP.R.3600	X		
SCAP.R.3800	X		
SCAP.R.3900	X		
SCAP.R.4000	X		
SCAP.R.4100	X		X
SCAP.R.4200		X	
SCAP.R.4300	X		
SCAP.R.4400		X	
SCAP.R.4500		X	

Appendix A—Terms and Definitions

This appendix lists definitions of key terms used in this document.

Authenticated Configuration Scanner: A product that runs with administrative or root privileges on a target system to conduct its assessment.

Automated Checklist: A checklist that is used through one or more tools that automatically alter or verify settings based on the contents of the checklist. Automated checklists document their security settings in a machine-readable format, either standard or proprietary.

CCE ID: An identifier for a specific configuration defined within the official CCE Dictionary and that conforms to the CCE specification. For more information please see the CCE specification reference in Section 2.

Checklist: A document that contains instructions or procedures for configuring an IT product to an operational environment, for verifying that the product has been configured properly, and/or for identifying unauthorized configuration changes to the product. Also referred to as a security configuration checklist, lockdown guide, hardening guide, security guide, security technical implementation guide (STIG), or benchmark.

Compliance Mapping: The process of correlating CCE settings defined in a source data stream with the security control identifiers defined in [NIST SP 800-53 R4].

CPE Name: An identifier for a unique uniform resource identifier (URI) assigned to a specific platform type that conforms to the CPE specification. For more information please see the CPE specification reference in Section 2.

CVE ID: An identifier for a specific software flaw defined within the official CVE Dictionary and that conforms to the CVE specification. For more information please see the CVE specification reference in Section 2.

Derived Test Requirement/Test Requirement: A statement of requirement, needed information, and associated test procedures necessary to test a specific SCAP feature.

Domain connected configuration: A test configuration whereby the Windows platform is joined to an Active Directory domain.

Import: A process available to end users by which an SCAP source data stream can be loaded into the vendor's product. During this process, the vendor process may optionally translate this file into a proprietary format.

Machine-Readable: Product output that is in a structured format, typically XML, which can be consumed by another program using consistent processing logic.

Major Revision: Any increase in the version of an SCAP component's specification or SCAP related data set that involves substantive changes that will break backwards compatibility with previous releases. See also *SCAP Revision*.

Minor Revision: Any increase in the version of an SCAP component's specification or SCAP related data set that may involve adding additional functionality, but that preserves backwards compatibility with previous releases. See also ***SCAP Revision***.

Misconfiguration: A setting within a computer program that violates a configuration policy or that permits or causes unintended behavior that impacts the security posture of a system. CCE can be used for enumerating misconfigurations.

> **NOTE:** NIST generally defines vulnerability as including both software flaws and configuration issues [misconfigurations]. For the purposes of the validation program and dependent procurement language, the SCAP Validation program is defining vulnerability and misconfiguration as two separate entities, with "vulnerability" referring strictly to software flaws.

Module (SCAP Module): it is an embedded software component of a product or application, or a complete product in-and-of-itself that has one or more capabilities.

National Checklist Program Repository (NCP): A NIST-maintained repository, which is a publicly available resource that contains information on a variety of security configuration checklists for specific IT products or categories of IT products.

National Vulnerability Database (NVD): The U.S. government repository of standards based vulnerability management data represented using the Security Content Automation Protocol (SCAP). This data informs automation of vulnerability management, security measurement, and compliance. NVD includes databases of security checklists, security related software flaws, misconfigurations, product names, and impact metrics.

Non-vendor-directed: This term is used to indicate that any sample chosen for testing is selected by the testing laboratory without the input or knowledge of the product vendor.

OVAL ID: An identifier for a specific OVAL definition that conforms to the format for OVAL IDs. For more information please see the OVAL specification reference in Section 2.

Product: A software application that has one or more capabilities.

Product Output: Information produced by a product. This includes the product user interface, human-readable reports, and machine-readable reports. Unless otherwise indicated by a specific requirement, there are no constraints on the format. When this output is evaluated in a test procedure, either all or specific forms of output will be sampled as indicated by the test procedure.

SCAP Capability: A specific function or functions of a product as defined below:

- Authenticated Configuration Scanner: the capability to audit and assess a target system to determine its compliance with a defined set of configuration requirements using target system logon privileges.

- Common Vulnerabilities and Exposures (CVE) Option: the capability to process and present CVEs correctly and completely.

- Open Checklist Interactive Language (OCIL) Option: the capability to process and present OCIL correctly and completely.

SCAP Component: One of the twelve specifications that comprise SCAP: Asset Identification, ARF, CCE, CCSS, CPE, CVE, CVSS, OCIL, OVAL, SWID, TMSAD, and XCCDF.

SCAP Result Data Stream: A bundle of SCAP components, along with the mappings of references between SCAP components, that holds output (result) content.

SCAP Revision: A version of the SCAP specification designated by a revision number in the format nn.nn.nn, where the first nn is the major revision number, the second nn number is the minor revision number, and the final nn number is the refinement number. A specific SCAP revision will populate all three fields, even if that means using zeros to show no minor revision or refinement number has been used to date. A leading zero will be used to pad single-digit revision or refinement numbers.

SCAP Source Data Stream: A bundle of SCAP components, along with the mappings of references between SCAP components, that holds input (source) content. See also **Compliance Mapping**.

Software Flaw: See **Checklist**.

Target Platform: The target operating system or application on which a vendor product will be evaluated using a platform-specific validation lab test suite. These platform-specific test suites consist of specialized SCAP content used to perform the test procedures defined in this document.

Vulnerability: An error, flaw, or mistake in computer software that permits or causes an unintended behavior to occur. CVE is a common means of enumerating vulnerabilities.

XCCDF Content: A file conforming to the XCCDF schema. For more information please see the XCCDF specification reference in Section 2.

Appendix B—Acronyms

This appendix contains selected acronyms and abbreviations used in the publication.

ACS	Authenticated Configuration Scanner
ARF	Asset Reporting Format
CCE	Common Configuration Enumeration
CCSS	Common Configuration Scoring System
CPE	Common Platform Enumeration
CVE	Common Vulnerabilities and Exposures
CVSS	Common Vulnerability Scoring System
DTR	Derived Test Requirement
FDCC	Federal Desktop Core Configuration
FIRST	Forum of Incident Response and Security Teams
FISMA	Federal Information Security Management Act
GUI	Graphical User Interface
HTML	Hypertext Markup Language
ID	Identifier
IETF	Internet Engineering Task Force
IR	Interagency Report
IT	Information Technology
ITL	Information Technology Laboratory
NCP	National Checklist Program
NIST	National Institute of Standards and Technology
NSA	National Security Agency
NVD	National Vulnerability Database
NVLAP	National Voluntary Laboratory Accreditation Program
OCIL	Open Checklist Interactive Language
OCIL QI	Open Checklist Interactive Language Questionnaire Interpreter
OMB	Office of Management and Budget
OS	Operating System
OVAL	Open Vulnerability and Assessment Language
OVAL DI	Open Vulnerability and Assessment Language Definition Interpreter
PDF	Portable Document Format
RFC	Request for Comment
RHEL	Red Hat Enterprise Linux
SCAP	Security Content Automation Protocol
SCAPVal	SCAP Validation tool
SP	Special Publication
SWID	Software Identification
TMSAD	Trust Model for Security Automation Data
URI	Uniform Resource Identifier
URL	Uniform Resource Locator
U.S.	United States
USGCB	United States Government Configuration Baseline
WFN	Well-Formed Name
XCCDF	Extensible Configuration Checklist Document Format
XML	Extensible Markup Language

Appendix C—Use of SCAP 1.3 Logo and phrases

This appendix contains information regarding the use of SCAP 1.3 Logo and phrases

The phrases SCAP 1.3 Validated and SCAP 1.3 Logo are intended for use in association with SCAP 1.3 products or modules validated by the National Institute of Standards and Technology (NIST) as complying with Security Content Automation Protocol (SCAP) Version 1.3 Requirements for Products/Modules.

Vendors of validated SCAP products and/or modules or vendors of products that embed validated SCAP modules are encouraged to use the phrases and logo provided that they agree to the following and returning the signed SCAP 1.3 Logo Form:

1. The phrases SCAP 1.3 Validated and the SCAP 1.3 Logo are Certification Marks of NIST, which retains exclusive rights to their use.

2. NIST reserves the right to control the quality of the use of the phrase SCAP 1.3 Validated and the logo itself.

3. Permission for advertising SCAP 1.3 validation and use of the logo is conditional on and limited to those SCAP products/modules validated by NIST as complying with the requirements for Security Content Automation Protocol (SCAP) Version 1.3.

4. An SCAP module may either be a component of a product, or a standalone product. Use of the SCAP 1.3 Logo on product reports, letterhead, brochures, marketing material, and product packaging SHALL be accompanied by the following: 'TM: A Certification Mark of NIST, which does not imply product endorsement by NIST or the U.S. Government'. If the SCAP module is a component of a product, the phrase "SCAP 1.3 Inside" SHALL accompany the logo.

5. Permission for the use of the phrase SCAP 1.3 Validated and the logo may be revoked at the discretion of NIST.

6. Permission to use the phrase SCAP 1.3 Validated and the SCAP 1.3 Logo in no way constitutes or implies product endorsement by NIST.

Appendix D—References

The following references are cited in the document above.

[FIPS 140-2]   Federal Information Process Standards Publication (FIPS) 140-2, *Security Requirements for Cryptographic Modules*, May 2001 (with Change Notices through December 3, 2002). https://doi.org/10.6028/NIST.FIPS.140-2.

[NIST HB 150]   NIST Handbook 150 (2006 Edition), *National Voluntary Laboratory Accreditation Program: Procedures and General Requirements*, February 2006. https://www.nist.gov/sites/default/files/documents/nvlap/nist-handbook-150.pdf.

[NIST HB 150-17]   NIST Handbook 150-17, *NVLAP Cryptographic and Security Testing*, May 2013. https://doi.org/10.6028/NIST.HB.150-17.

[NISTIR 7275 R4]   NIST Interagency Report (NISTIR) 7275 Revision 4, *Specification for the Extensible Configuration Checklist Description Format (XCCDF) Version 2.1*, September 2011 (updated March 2012). https://csrc.nist.gov/publications/detail/nistir/7275/rev-4/final.

[NISTIR 7502]   NIST Interagency Report (NISTIR) 7502, *The Common Configuration Scoring System (CCSS): Metrics for Software Security Configuration Vulnerabilities*, December 2010. https://doi.org/10.6028/NIST.IR.7502.

[NISTIR 7511 R3]   NIST Interagency Report (NISTIR) 7511 Revision 3, *Security Content Automation Protocol (SCAP) Version 1.2 Validation Program Test Requirements*, January 2013 (updated July 11, 2013). https://doi.org/10.6028/NIST.IR.7511.

[NISTIR 7511 R4]   NIST Interagency Report (NISTIR) 7511 Revision 4, *Security Content Automation Protocol (SCAP) Version 1.2 Validation Program Test Requirements*, January 2016. https://doi.org/10.6028/NIST.IR.7511r4.

[NISTIR 7692]   NIST Interagency Report (NISTIR) 7692, *Specification for the Open Checklist Interactive Language (OCIL) Version 2.0*, April 2011. https://doi.org/10.6028/NIST.IR.7692.

[NISTIR 7693]   NIST Interagency Report (NISTIR) 7693, *Specification for Asset Identification 1.1*, June 2011. https://doi.org/10.6028/NIST.IR.7693.

[NISTIR 7694]   NIST Interagency Report (NISTIR) 7694, *Specification for the Asset Reporting Format 1.1*, June 2011. https://doi.org/10.6028/NIST.IR.7694.

[NISTIR 7695]   NIST Interagency Report (NISTIR) 7695, *Common Platform Enumeration: Naming Specification Version 2.3*, August 2011. https://doi.org/10.6028/NIST.IR.7695.

[NISTIR 7696]   NIST Interagency Report (NISTIR) 7696, *Common Platform Enumeration: Name Matching Specification Version 2.3*, August 2011. https://doi.org/10.6028/NIST.IR.7696.

[NISTIR 7697]   NIST Interagency Report (NISTIR) 7697, *Common Platform Enumeration: Dictionary Specification Version 2.3*, August 2011.
https://doi.org/10.6028/NIST.IR.7697.

[NISTIR 7698]   NIST Interagency Report (NISTIR) 7698, *Common Platform Enumeration: Applicability Language Specification Version 2.3*, August 2011.
https://doi.org/10.6028/NIST.IR.7698.

[NISTIR 7802]   NIST Interagency Report (NISTIR) 7802, *Trust Model for Security Automation Data 1.0 (TMSAD)*, September 2011.
https://doi.org/10.6028/NIST.IR.7802.

[NIST SP 800-126 R1]   NIST Special Publication (SP) 800-126 Revision 1, *The Technical Specification for the Security Content Automation Protocol (SCAP): SCAP Version 1.1*, February 2011.
https://doi.org/10.6028/NIST.SP.800-126r1.

[NIST SP 800-126 R2]   NIST Special Publication (SP) 800-126 Revision 2, *The Technical Specification for the Security Content Automation Protocol (SCAP): SCAP Version 1.2*, September 2011.
https://doi.org/10.6028/NIST.SP.800-126r2.

[NIST SP 800-126 R3]   NIST Special Publication (SP) 800-126 Revision 3, *The Technical Specification for the Security Content Automation Protocol (SCAP): SCAP Version 1.3*, February 2018.
https://doi.org/10.6028/NIST.SP.800-126r3.

[NIST SP 800-126A]   NIST Special Publication (SP) 800-126A, *SCAP 1.3 Component Specification Version Updates: An Annex to NIST Special Publication 800-126 Revision 3*, February 2018.
https://doi.org/10.6028/NIST.SP.800-126A.

[NIST SP 800-53 R4]   NIST Special Publication (SP) 800-53 Revision 4, *Security and Privacy Controls for Federal Information Systems and Organizations*, April 2013 (updated January 22, 2015).
https://doi.org/10.6028/NIST.SP.800-53r4.

[NIST SP 800-70 R4]   NIST Special Publication (SP) 800-70 Revision 4, *National Checklist Program for IT Products – Guidelines for Checklist Users and Developers*, February 2018.
https://doi.org/10.6028/NIST.SP.800-70r4.

[OMB M-08-22]   Office of Management and Budget (OMB) Memorandum M-08-22, *Guidance on the Federal Desktop Core Configuration (FDCC)*, August 11, 2008.
https://georgewbush-whitehouse.archives.gov/omb/memoranda/fy2008/m08-22.pdf.

[RFC 2119]   Internet Engineering Task Force (IETF) Request for Comment (RFC) 2119, *Key words for use in RFCs to Indicate Requirement Levels*, March 1997.
https://doi.org/10.17487/RFC2119.

[SWID]   ISO/IEC 19770-2:2015, *Information technology – Software asset management – Part 2: Software identification tag*, October 2015 (corrected March 2017).
http://www.iso.org/iso/catalogue_detail.htm?csnumber=65666.

[XMLS]   World Wide Web Consortium (W3C) Recommendation, *XML Schema* [XML Schema 1.1], October 28, 2004.
http://www.w3.org/XML/Schema.html.

www.ingramcontent.com/pod-product-compliance
Lightning Source LLC
LaVergne TN
LVHW060148070326
832902LV00018B/3011